SQUIRREL

A Nature Story b

Illustrated by Marjorie Blamey

COLLINS COLOUR CUBS

Squirrel Wood stretched from Cock Robin's garden to Frog's Pond, covering the entire slope along one side of Woodmouse Lane. Most of it was pinewood, mixed with silver birches. The remainder was a mixture of oak, beech and horse chestnut, with a border of hazels along the bottom of the slope.

There were, of course, other creatures in the wood besides squirrels, and some of them, like the owls, woodpeckers, roe deer and badgers, lived there all the time.

Squirrel was a red squirrel,
and had been born in
the pinewood, where he
still lived with his mate
and others of his own
kind. He was a pinewood
squirrel. Pine trees suited his way
of life best, and he seldom visited
other parts of the wood.

The nest of a squirrel is called a
drey. Squirrel's sleeping drey was
built high in a pine tree, in a narrow
fork against the main stem, and
was bigger than a football. Other
branches grew from the fork, giving
the drey a secure cradle. Squirrel
had made the drey himself, using old
twigs and grass and bits of bark,
all tightly woven together. The
inside was padded with moss, dead
leaves and bark, and was very snug.
There were many other such nests in
pine trees in other parts of the wood.

There was no special entrance to the
drey, such as wrens have to their domed
nests. When squirrel wanted in, he
scraped and bored his way through the
outer covering, sealing it behind him.
On the way out he did the same.

During the worst days of the winter
Squirrel's mate lived with him in his
drey, where they cuddled together,
keeping each other warm. Even when
the drey was roofed with snow they slept
warm, and when the thaw came not a
drop of water seeped into the cosy nest.
But, unlike the dormouse and the hedge-
hog, they did *not* hibernate: they merely
stayed indoors when the day was too
wet or windy.

Squirrel and his mate
stayed in the nest on
stormy days of rain or
snow, or when a gale was
blowing, but on other
days they were out and
about as usual.

With the coming of spring Squirrel's mate drove him out of the drey, because she was expecting a family and wanted it to herself. She carried in moss and leaves, and added new twigs and bark to the outside, making it bigger.

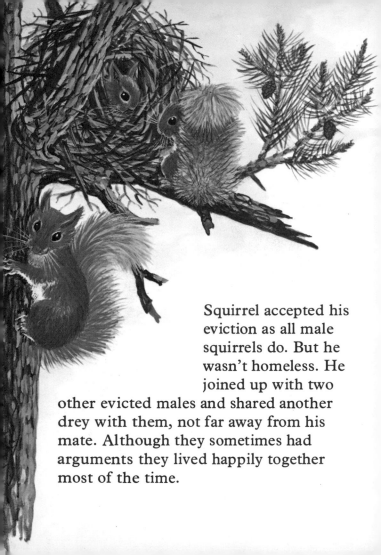

Squirrel accepted his
eviction as all male
squirrels do. But he
wasn't homeless. He
joined up with two
other evicted males and shared another
drey with them, not far away from his
mate. Although they sometimes had
arguments they lived happily together
most of the time.

By now Squirrel's coat had faded a great
deal, and his bushy tail had bleached
almost to the colour of straw. At this
period he spent a lot of his time on the
ground, scraping in search of food he
had buried the previous autumn. Sometimes he found a store by chance; more
often he located it with his nose. It
is unlikely that he remembered exactly
where he had hidden anything, or even
if the store he dug up was his own or
some other squirrel's.
All he knew was that
he would be sure to
find food if he kept
on digging.

The squirrels didn't
have the wood to them-
selves. Always there
were the roe deer, who
came out in the even-
ing to feed about the
time the squirrels were
going to bed.

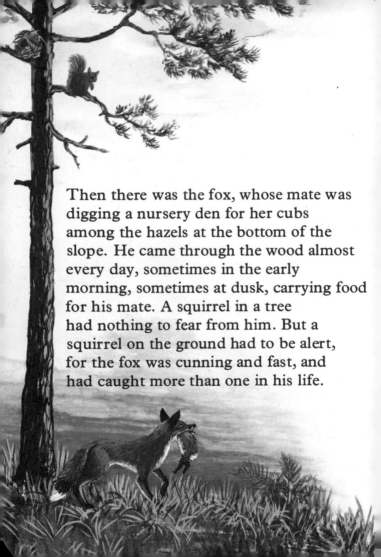

Then there was the fox, whose mate was digging a nursery den for her cubs among the hazels at the bottom of the slope. He came through the wood almost every day, sometimes in the early morning, sometimes at dusk, carrying food for his mate. A squirrel in a tree had nothing to fear from him. But a squirrel on the ground had to be alert, for the fox was cunning and fast, and had caught more than one in his life.

Squirrel knew
both roe deer
and fox because
he had seen
them in the wood
during the day.
But the badgers
he knew almost
nothing about,
because they
came out after
dusk when all the squirrels were in
their nests. Squirrel had only twice
in his life seen a badger, and that was
when he was getting out of bed, and the
badger was hurrying to be home before
sunrise. For the same reason the badger
knew nothing about squirrels as he had
never seen one in his whole life.

In most years the long-eared owls reared
their young in the old nest of a crow.
But this year the hen owl trampled flat
an old drey for a nest and laid five
eggs in it. Although the owls were
night birds, Squirrel often saw the hen
on the nest during the day.

Squirrel knew the
woodpeckers well.
They were noisy
birds and seemed
always to be flying
about wherever
he happened to be.
Each year they
drilled a new
nesting hole under
a bracket fungus,
in an old peeling
birch tree near
Squirrel's drey.
He was always
curious about
what they were doing, but if
he tried to peep into their
nesting hole they flew at him
angrily and drove him away.
They had every reason to chase
him for he would very likely
have eaten their eggs.

The jays ate the same sort of food as the squirrels for much of the year, but they also hunted insects, snails, worms and mice, and in spring they raided birds' nests. One day Squirrel watched a jay stealing the eggs of a wood-pigeon.

Although Squirrel liked pine cones more than anything else, he also ate a great variety of fruits, nuts, seeds, buds and shoots, according to the time of year. When he wanted a change he hunted for insects and their larvae. Like the jays he sometimes raided the nests of small birds, eating eggs and nestlings. If he found an old bone of some long-dead rabbit or deer he would sometimes gnaw at it and eat a little for the *Calcium*. But you must not think he was an eater of bones.

As the spring wore on Squirrel's whole appearance began to change. His red summer fur had now grown in as far as his hips, but he still had the thick fluffy winter fur on his hindquarters. So for a time he looked as though he were wearing baggy trousers. The squirrels were now feeding on oak and chestnut catkins, as well as green pine cones which they shredded and ate as readily as they did ripe ones.

Squirrel seldom drank water, because he
usually got all he needed from food and
dew. But by the time he was in his summer
coat the weather had become dry and hot,
so he travelled with other squirrels to
a small pool under the oaks. Round the
edge of the pool the water was dusty
with yellow pine pollen.

On one of his visits to the pool he met
two of the grey squirrels who lived in
that part of the wood. They were bigger
and heavier animals than Squirrel, and
much stronger, but they paid hardly any
attention to him, even when he began to
drink almost alongside them. The grey
squirrels were Americans—descendants
of American squirrels brought to
Britain in 1876 and in later years.

Squirrel's mate allowed him back near her nest when she had weaned her young. On their first day out, Squirrel watched them from a higher branch where he was nibbling a cone. They weren't very agile yet, and were scared of everything that moved.

But their confidence grew day
by day, and before long they
were as active in the branches
as Squirrel himself.

They chased each other along
the highest branches and
round and round the main
trunk. Their long claws gave
them a sure grip, and saved
them many a time when it
seemed one of them must fall.

Squirrel had his favourite perches, where he liked to sit when he was eating. One of his perches was on top of the wood-peckers' nesting tree, where he often sat nib-bling pine cones; the ground below, and round about, was soon littered with the cores. Another of his perches was an old pine stump in a clearing, but he didn't use it as often as the woodpeckers' tree. And even the woodpeckers' tree wasn't his favourite place.

His favourite eating place was
a big pine tree, on a stout
branch close to the trunk,
and this was the perch he
could be seen on at some time
almost every day. He always
climbed to it by the same
route, and the bark below it
was worn almost bare by his
hindclaws. The ground litter
of cores was greater here
than at any of his other
eating places.

Early one morning he was on his pine stump in the clearing when he saw the movement of a fox in a thicket on the edge. Squirrel dropped the cone he had been gnawing, leaped from the stump, and went bounding across the open to the nearest pine tree. He was six feet up the trunk when the fox reached the bottom, snapping his jaws, but it was a narrow escape, and it took Squirrel the rest of the day to recover from the fright.

The following afternoon he was on the woodpeckers' tree, reaching down to nibble at a fungus, when the young woodpeckers left the nesting hole and began circling the trunk below him, gripping the bark securely with their strong claws as expertly as baby squirrels.

Another day he was
climbing to his pine perch
when he noticed that it
was occupied by a
strange shape. The
shape looked like a
length of rolled bark,
and that's what
Squirrel thought it was
until the long-eared
owl opened one eye.
The owl stayed there
until dark, keeping
Squirrel off it all day.

Summer was a time of ever-increasing food supply and Squirrel made almost daily forays into other parts of the wood in search of new titbits. He stripped tender twigs of beech, oak and sycamore. He nibbled at the tiny acorns forming on the oak twigs. On the slope he ate the sweet, juicy fruits of the wild raspberries, and the first blackberries on the brambles.

In early August Squirrel
saw the roe deer every
morning about the time he
was leaving his drey to
search for food.

It was now the roe deer's mating time,
and Squirrel watched the buck chasing
the doe in rings round the woodpeckers'
tree.

Squirrel's busiest time of the year
came when the wild harvest was ripe or
ripening, and he spent several hours
on many days gathering acorns in the
oakwood, eating some on the spot and
carrying away others in his mouth.

Besides acorns, he gathered beech nuts, which are known as *mast*. He chiselled through the tough clasps of the shell with his teeth to reach the seeds inside. On his first visit he ate his fill of seeds in the tree, but later on he collected the whole nuts and carried them to the pinewood. Some he stored in an old nest-hole in the woodpeckers' tree; others he hid in the ground all over the clearing.

Then he began carry- ing acorns from the oakwood. It is com- monly believed that squirrels lay up big stores of food in a few places. The truth is they hide a little food in many places—mostly buried in the ground.

The hazel nuts
weren't quite ripe
but Squirrel
tasted one and
found it to his
liking, so he
picked another,
and another, gnawed through the shells
and ate the kernels on the spot. But
he didn't carry any away. That he
would do later, when the nuts were hard
and brown, and ready for storing.

From now on he buried
more food in the ground
than he hid anywhere
else, scraping shallow
holes with his forepaws,
then covering his store
over with loose earth and
leaves. In these caches
he hid acorns, hazel nuts,
beech mast, pine cones,
doghips, haws and
rowan-berries. During these
days he seemed to be
forever digging.

He was gathering
acorns one day when
a grey squirrel
rushed at him.

It chased him into the
highest branches, and in
the end forced him to make
a wild leap into another
tree.

That experience taught Squirrel a
lesson, and he remained more than a
little afraid of the bigger American
greys. From that day he was careful
not to mix with them, or approach them
too closely. The greys were busy har-
vesting and resented the reds because
they were competitors, collecting the
same kind of food.

Soon all the squirrels were gathering and storing food, mostly in holes in the ground. They buried it on the slope, in the oakwood, and in the pinewood, always scraping in a different place, so that no squirrel dug up another squirrel's hoard. The squirrels would forget where they had buried some of their stores, but they would find enough of them again to keep them alive in the lean days ahead.

Besides cones, nuts and seeds there
were now other foods in the wood which
the squirrels liked to eat, but hardly
ever bothered trying to store. These
were the fungi, which were now plentiful.
The fungi are the family of mushrooms
and toadstools, and one that all
the squirrels liked very much
was the *Agaric*. Squirrel
nibbled Agaric quite a
lot and hid a few pieces in
the ground.

Another mushroom the squirrels liked very much was the *Boletus*, which was much bigger than the Agaric. Squirrel usually nibbled at a fat Boletus, but sometimes he pushed one over and bit out pieces which he carried away. Some of the pieces he buried in the ground, but he wedged other bits in cracks on the trunk of his favourite pine tree, as he had already done with a few nuts and acorns.

A jay came to bury acorns near the spot where Squirrel was burying hazel nuts. Between the jay and Squirrel was a group of small oak trees, which had grown from acorns buried by squirrels and jays in earlier years, and forgotten about. When an oakwood spreads uphill it usually grows from acorns planted by jays and squirrels, because acorns can't roll uphill.

Even the youngest squirrels were
collecting and hiding food, which meant
that they had to spend a lot of time
on the ground. Although they were
sharp-eyed and alert, they were not as
wary as the old ones, and one day a
kestrel swooped and killed one while it
was running in the open with a hazel
nut. The other squirrels fled to the
safety of the trees, while the kestrel
flapped into the air with the young
squirrel dangling from a foot.

Squirrel was now sharing a drey with
his mate again, and when the storms
came, with sleet or rain or snow, they
slept warm together. They had stored
a lot of food so they were never hungry.
All they had to do was scrape in the
ground to find a meal, if they didn't
want to sit in high branches during
windy or rainy days.

In winter, even when there was snow on the ground, Squirrel and his mate came out nearly every day to visit their stores. They found the hidden food with their noses, rather than by memory, and it is quite likely that, as often as not, they dug up some other squirrel's store.

You must never imagine that the squirrel
is a sleepy-head who spends most of
the winter asleep in his nest. Only
the very worst weather keeps him indoors.

ISBN 0 00 123285 1
Text copyright © 1978 David Stephen
Illustrations copyright © 1978 Marjorie Blamey
Printed and made in Great Britain